Blue Animals

by Teddy Borth

ABDO
ANIMAL COLORS
Kids

abdopublishing.com

Published by Abdo Kids, a division of ABDO, PO Box 398166, Minneapolis, Minnesota 55439.

Copyright © 2015 by Abdo Consulting Group, Inc. International copyrights reserved in all countries. No part of this book may be reproduced in any form without written permission from the publisher.

Printed in the United States of America, North Mankato, Minnesota.

102014

012015

Photo Credits: Corbis, iStock, Shutterstock, Thinkstock

Production Contributors: Teddy Borth, Jennie Forsberg, Grace Hansen

Design Contributors: Candice Keimig, Laura Rask, Dorothy Toth

Library of Congress Control Number: 2014943666

Cataloging-in-Publication Data

Borth, Teddy.

 Blue animals / Teddy Borth.

   p. cm. -- (Animal colors)

ISBN 978-1-62970-694-8 (lib. bdg.)

Includes index.

1. Animals--Juvenile literature.   I. Title.

590--dc23

                        2014943666

Table of Contents

Blue

Blue is a **primary color**.

Blue cannot be made

by mixing other colors.

Mixing Colors

● + ○ = ●

○ + ● = ●

● + ● = ●

● + ● + ● = ●

Primary Colors

● Red

○ Yellow

● Blue

Secondary Colors

● Orange

● Green

● Purple

5

Blue on Land

The Sinai agama is a lizard.
It can change its color. It uses
blue to get a female's attention.

6

Young blue slugs are
brown. They turn blue
when they become adults.

9

British shorthair cats come in many colors. Blue was so popular it got its own name. It is called "British Blue."

Blue in Air

Male peafowls are called peacocks. Males have bright blue bodies. Females like the large feathers.

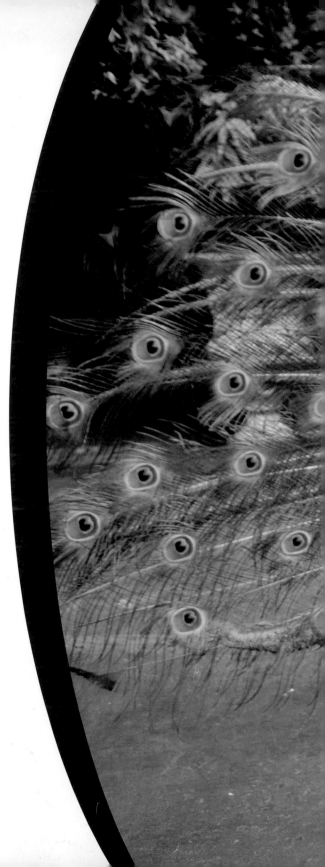

The Hyacinth Macaw is a parrot.

Its feathers are blue. It is the

world's largest flying parrot.

A morpho butterfly is blue.
Morpho means "changed." It is
a metallic blue color. Its blue
changes **shades** as it moves.

Blue in Water

Only male ribbon eels
are blue. They can grow
a yard (1 m) long.

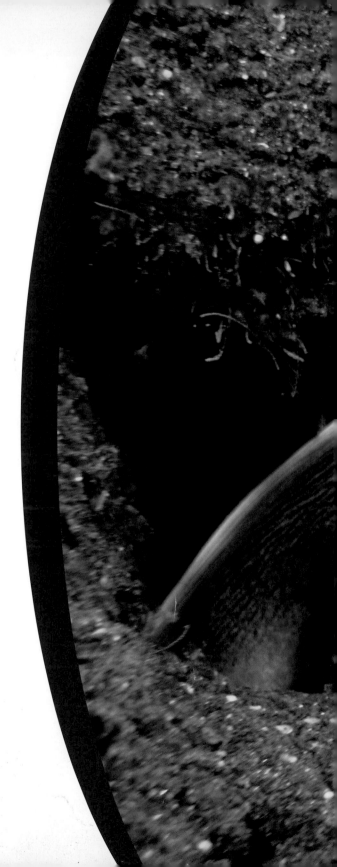

One in two million

lobsters are blue. Their

color is the only difference.

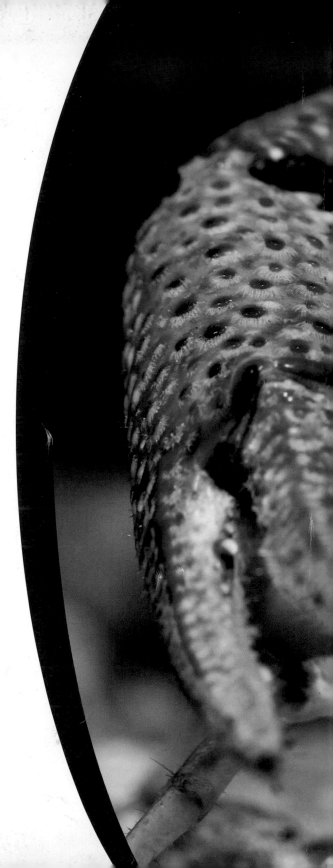

More Facts

- Blue is the most popular color in the United States and Europe. It was chosen by half of both men and women.

- 17% of people in the United States have blue eyes. In the country of **Estonia**, 99% of people have blue eyes.

- Blue is the color of ice, cold, sadness, **harmony**, faithfulness, and **confidence**.

Glossary

confidence – a feeling of trust in someone or something.

Estonia – a country in northern Europe. It is south of Finland. It borders Latvia and Russia.

harmony – peace.

primary color – a color that cannot be made by mixing other colors.

secondary color – a color resulting from mixing two primary colors.

shade – a darker or lighter version of a color.

Index

abdokids.com

Use this code to log on to abdokids.com and access crafts, games, videos, and more!

Abdo Kids Code:
ABK6948